100CLASSIC**METAL**
LICKSFOR**GUITAR**

Learn 100 Rock & Metal Guitar Licks in The Style Of The World's Greatest Players

CHRIS**ZOUPA**

FUNDAMENTAL**CHANGES**

100 Classic Metal Licks For Guitar

Learn 100 Rock & Metal Guitar Licks in The Style Of The World's Greatest Players

ISBN: 978-1-78933-464-7

Published by **www.fundamental-changes.com**

Copyright © 2025 Chris Zoupa

Edited by Joseph Alexander

www.fundamental-changes.com

@fundamentalchanges

Join our free Facebook Community of Cool Musicians

www.facebook.com/groups/fundamentalguitar

For over 350 free guitar lessons with Videos, check out:

www.fundamental-changes.com

Cover Image: Artwork for Electric Bears for Fundamental Changes Ltd.

Contents

Introduction

Welcome to *100 Classic Metal Licks For Guitar*, your one-stop-shop into the wild world of legendary metal guitarists, their insane techniques, and the licks that made them gods among mortals. If you've ever wondered how Randy Rhoads managed to make arpeggios sound like Beethoven on a booze-up, or how Kirk Hammett can turn two notes into a masterpiece of vibrato angst then, my friend, you've come to the right place.

What are we covering? Oh, just 100 licks in the style of the world's greatest metal guitarists!

You're going to learn all about the unique styles and techniques of guitar icons like Eddie Van Halen, Zakk Wylde, Marty Friedman, Nuno Bettencourt and more. From pentatonic fury and screaming harmonics, to legato runs that will make your fingers question their loyalty to your brain… this book is packed with everything you need to emulate the styles of your favourite big-hair shredders

By the time you're done here, you'll take your playing from "I can sorta stumble through Master of Puppets if no one's watching" to "I can bust out licks so fiery they make other guitarists question their life choices (and mine!)" This book isn't for beginners, it's for players who already know their way around the fretboard and want to add some serious sizzle to their solos. Think of it as the secret sauce that will transform your playing from solid to absolutely face-melting.

The idea is that, by the end of this book, you'll…

- Bend notes like Dimebag (with extra aggression and scary facial expressions)

- Add flashy taps and whammy dives that'd make Eddie Van-Jealous

- Throw in chromatic chaos and unexpected notes to keep people guessing, *à la* Kirk

- Play solos that are equal parts melodic and chaotic, like Marty does on every Megadeth album that ever mattered

- Play double-stops and bluesy bends that Slash would approve of (hat and sunglasses optional)

But this isn't just about learning cool licks. It's about why these licks work, how these players approached their solos, and how to make these techniques your own. You'll come out of this not just copying your heroes but understanding how they think (or at least how they thought when they weren't partying until 4.00am in some forgotten corner of LA).

This book is for anyone who wants to play faster, shred harder, and sound more like themselves in the process. It's also for anyone who appreciates the occasional ridiculous aside and brutal honesty about what it takes to improve as a guitarist.

Let's face it, metal guitar is a brutal, unforgiving art form, but it's also ridiculously fun. So grab your guitar, plug in and let's get started. Just don't blame me if you blow out your amp halfway through Chapter Three – that's on you!

Have fun!

Chris

Get the Audio

The audio files for this book are available to download for free from **www.fundamental-changes.com.** The link is in the top right-hand corner. Click on the "Guitar" link then simply select this book title from the drop-down menu and follow the instructions to get the audio.

We recommend that you download the files directly to your computer, not to your tablet, and extract them there before that adds them to your media library.

For over 350 free guitar lessons with videos check out:

www.fundamental-changes.com

Join our free Facebook Community of Cool Musicians

www.facebook.com/groups/fundamentalguitar

Tag us for a share on Instagram: **FundamentalChanges**

Chapter One – Ace Frehley

Paul Daniel "Ace" Frehley was born in 1951 in New York City, USA. He is also known by several other monikers including, *The Celestial One*, *Mr Excitement*, and, most famously among diehard KISS fans, simply as *Spaceman*.

Ace got his first electric guitar at the age of 14. He cites The Rolling Stones, Jimi Hendrix, Buddy Guy, B.B. King, Albert King and, of course, Led Zeppelin, as his earliest musical influences. However, he considers Pete Townshend his favourite guitarist of all time.

I didn't make the connection between Ace and Pete until I watched footage of The Who in their prime. Townshend's stage presence, his iconic use of the "kill switch" sound between pickup selectors, and countless other techniques undoubtedly helped shape the mega-rock-star Ace Frehley would become.

At the start of his musical journey, Frehley played in cover bands and various small-time groups. However, his career trajectory changed drastically when he answered a newspaper ad in early 1973.

The then-unnamed band posted an ad that read: "Band seeking a lead guitarist with flash & balls" and flash and balls he had. Ace's audition in front of Gene Simmons and Paul Stanley was a success, securing him a place in what would become the first and most iconic lineup of KISS.

KISS released their self-titled debut album in 1974, featuring hits like *Strutter* and *Nothin' to Lose*, both of which include outstanding guitar solos. These singles, along with the album as a whole, cemented Ace as one of the most exciting new guitar heroes of the 1970s.

Ace saw tremendous success during his nine-year run with KISS, particularly with their KISS ALIVE album. It was the band's fourth release and their first live album, showcasing their electrifying stage show, stellar live sound, and impressive catalogue of songs. To date, the album has sold a staggering 9 million copies.

Ace Frehley is famously associated with his signature Les Paul Custom guitar equipped with three cream-colored humbuckers. Like many rockers of his era, he was also a loyal user of Marshall amplifiers.

Guitar heroes from the 1980s, 1990s, and even the modern day often cite Ace Frehley as a key inspiration. The list of admirers is long, including Dimebag Darrell (Pantera), John 5 (Rob Zombie, Mötley Crüe, solo work), Scott Ian (Anthrax), and Tom Morello (Audioslave, Rage Against the Machine) – all of whom were devoted KISS fans. Alongside Paul Stanley, Ace inspired a generation of guitarists who went on to form bands, release groundbreaking albums, and create some of the most iconic moments in Rock 'n' Roll history.

One of the most iconic Ace Frehley quotes I've come across is, "I'm always flattered when people tell me I influenced them. If I knew I was gonna influence thousands of guitar players, I woulda practiced more."

Recommended Listening

KISS – *Hotter Than Hell (1974)*

KISS – *Destroyer (1976)*

KISS – *Love Gun (1977)*

Ace Frehley – *Self Titled (1978)*

Frehley's Comet – *Second Sighting (1988)*

All the licks in this chapter will be played over a KISS '70s rock style backing track in B Dorian.

We'll start with a lick that uses the B Minor Pentatonic scale, featuring Ace's signature triplet legato bursts. These quick hammer-ons and pull-offs, a staple of countless KISS solos, are a great way to add excitement to your pentatonic playing without a lot of extra effort.

The lick resolves in the fourth shape of B Minor Pentatonic and uses sustained double-stop bends. For the 17th fret bend, try using your ring finger, with your pinkie placed on the 17th fret of the first string underneath. You can also use your middle and ring fingers, but this might feel a bit cramped.

Example 1a:

In the next lick, we'll mix alternate picking with legato. Start with four picked 1/16th notes, then follow with one picked note leading into a rolling legato triplet. You'll notice how shifting between these techniques creates a burst of speed as the rhythm moves from straight 1/16ths to triplet 1/16ths.

One of the great things about this lick is its consistency – the rolling legato pattern is the same across the first, second, and third strings. It's a clever way to bring a fresh twist to the pentatonic scale, incorporating extra flavour from the 2nd, major 6th, and b5 intervals.

Example 1b:

Now, let's move on to a wide vibrato lick in a 1/4 note triplet pulse. This is a great way to make your vibrato more expressive and distinctive, moving beyond simple note-sustaining.

Technically, this isn't really vibrato – it's more like a repeating whole-tone bend. To get this right, you'll need to control each bend carefully to hit the target note consistently. Use your ring finger to bend, with the other two fingers supporting behind it, and add some wrist motion to help with power.

The lick wraps up with a high pentatonic run featuring 1/16th notes, legato and bends. To play this, try barring the first and second strings and using outside picking. Pay close attention to the picking patterns in the third and fourth bars.

Example 1c:

This next lick builds on some legato rolls within the pentatonic scale, spiced up with open strings for added flair.

If the key you're playing in allows for open strings, it's always worth experimenting with that. Adding open string notes can elevate even the simplest pentatonic idea, bringing an extra layer of speed and surprise.

Example 1d:

Next, we'll explore a lick based on Ace's iconic wide, controlled bends. It's written as three 1/16th notes tied together so that each phase of the bend – rest, up, and down – gets equal weight and clarity.

If you're struggling with the phrasing, check out the audio examples – they're a big help if you get stuck.

Example 1e:

Here, we'll dive into a fast two-string legato lick. At full speed, you might find it easier to barre the 19th fret for smoother execution.

In the final two bars, you'll encounter a surprise major 3rd on the 8th fret of the G string. Using a major 3rd in a predominantly minor context is a fantastic way to grab the listener's attention. This technique has been used by legends like Jimi Hendrix, Dimebag Darrell, SRV, and Slash.

Example 1f:

Now we'll look at a lick that combines the first shape B Minor Pentatonic box with legato, played vertically across two bars. The repeating pattern alternates between four legato notes and one picked note. Focus on keeping your legato notes even in volume, and follow up with a sharp staccato 1/8th note for contrast.

The lick then shifts into the third and fourth pentatonic shapes, combining legato and slides. You can play this part almost entirely with your pointer and ring fingers, making it a great exercise for strengthening those fingers, particularly in a legato context.

Example 1g:

Next is a classic Ace Frehley move: repeating a three-note-per-string shape across four strings. This works as long as it aligns with the first shape pentatonic box of the key you're playing in. Adding an extra note to each string introduces the 2nd, major 6th, b5, and b2 (or b9), creating more tension and harmonic variety.

The lick resolves with some chromatic phrases on the second string that mix picking and legato. Try to anticipate the legato pull-offs and roll all three fingers across the notes smoothly.

Example 1h:

This idea focuses on double-stops and Ace's signature staccato attack. Play the double-stops with a flat pointer finger and execute the bends with your ring finger, using your middle finger as support. Adding a wrist-twisting motion can help with control.

You can hear this style of "stabby" phrasing in KISS solos like *I Was Made For Lovin' You* and *Black Diamond*. It also reflects Chuck Berry's influence on Ace's playing.

Example 1i:

Lastly, here's a lick that combines percussive dead notes, double-stops, and Ace's signature 1½-step bends. Both techniques are essential to Ace's style, so we'll break them down step by step.

Start by controlling the dampened notes for a percussive effect. Rest your pointer finger loosely over the 7th fret while lightly resting your other fingers on the strings. Lift off slightly between the dead notes to articulate the double-stops.

For the bends in the third and fourth bars, you'll need to dig in. Use three fingers for support, twist your wrist, and maybe even lift your shoulder slightly to reach the target note with precision and attitude.

Example 1j:

Chapter Two – Randy Rhoads

Randall William Rhoads, better known as "Randy," was born in 1956 in Santa Monica, California, USA. At the age of 7, he began piano and classical guitar lessons at the music school his mother owned. This early foundation of theory, classical appreciation and discipline would go on to shape Randy's signature sound – a fusion of heavy metal and classical music that defined his tragically short career.

Randy cited guitar heroes like Ritchie Blackmore, Michael Schenker (UFO), and John Williams as major influences on his playing. His musical tastes weren't rigid, and he showed a genuine appreciation for multiple genres.

Blackmore's influence is especially evident in Randy's ability to blend heavy metal with classical motifs, a hallmark of his style. Blackmore had pioneered this fusion in his work with Deep Purple and Rainbow from the late 1960s to the mid-1970s. This laid the groundwork for what would later become "neo-classical metal," a genre Randy helped propel alongside artists like Jason Becker and Yngwie Malmsteen.

Randy's first serious band, Quiet Riot, was formed in 1973 while he was still a teenager. Their debut album, *Quiet Riot*, was released in 1978. Despite gaining local buzz and popularity the band struggled to secure a U.S. record deal and ultimately signed with a Japanese label. While this limited their early commercial success in America, it helped establish the band, and Randy, as a powerhouse in rock, known for catchy choruses and exceptional guitar work.

By the late 1970s, Randy's growing reputation as a guitarist rivalled that of Eddie Van Halen. The two were often compared, with fans and critics pitting their tapping, shredding, cross-handed bends, and whammy bar tricks against each other. This rivalry didn't go unnoticed. Recently fired Black Sabbath vocalist Ozzy Osbourne, looking to launch a solo career, took note. Randy was brought on board and together they recorded and toured two classic albums before his untimely death in 1982.

Randy's signature guitar, the Jackson Rhoads Concord, was his re-imagining of the traditional, symmetrical Gibson Flying V. His design was smaller, with a thinner, more shark-finned or arrow-like appearance. During its prototype phase, Randy sketched his idea on a napkin and shared it with Grover Jackson. That napkin sketch ultimately became one of the most iconic guitars of the last century.

Like many rock guitar heroes of the '70s and '80s, Randy predominantly used Marshall amplifiers both live and in the studio.

The combination of V-style guitars and Marshall amps wasn't groundbreaking in itself. What made Randy's sound unique was his note choice, skill, and the distinct way he double-tracked his solos. By intentionally creating slightly imperfect doubles, he introduced dissonance, humanisation, and an edge of chaos that became a signature element of his playing.

Over the years, countless guitar heroes, including Michael Romeo, Paul Gilbert, Mick Thomson, Alexi Laiho, Tom Morello, Phil X, and Zakk Wylde, have praised Randy for his contributions to heavy metal, the neo-classical genre, and he has inspired generations of young guitarists worldwide.

In 2021, Randy Rhoads was posthumously inducted into the Rock and Roll Hall of Fame by Rage Against the Machine's Tom Morello. During his speech, Tom delivered a poignant tribute:

"In a way, Randy Rhoads is the Robert Johnson of metal. It's such a small catalogue of stuff that has been so incredibly influential."

Randy's humility and passion for music were reflected in his ethos. A quote that perfectly captures his outlook is,

"There's no reason for a guitarist to have a big ego. You should love the instrument more than wanting to be a rock star."

Recommended Listening

Quiet Riot – *Quiet Riot (1978)*

Quiet Riot – *Quiet Riot II (1978)*

Ozzy Osbourne – *Blizzard of Ozz (1980)*

Ozzy Osbourne – *Diary of a Madman (1981)*

The Randy Rhoads-themed licks I've put together for this chapter are designed to be played over an Ozzy Osbourne glam style backing track in F# Minor.

In the first of ten licks, you'll use the C# Phrygian CAGED shape to explore some variations of a descending diatonic lick. It features a mix of legato and subdivision switching, which keeps things both fun and challenging.

Pay special attention to the legato emphasis at the start of bars one and three – it's all too easy to speed through this bit. Take your time, and if you're unsure about the phrasing, give the audio example a good listen.

Example 2a:

Next, we'll look at an F# Minor Pentatonic lick based around the first shape box but in the high octave.

This one's all about speed, with a triplet 1/16th-note emphasis that'll have your fingers flying. The picking might feel a bit frantic at first, but using economy picking (think mini-sweeps) can really help with the string crossings in bar one. Don't forget to check the notation. There are two up-picks marked that are easy to miss!

The lick resolves in bar four with a C# major arpeggio, spiced up by Randy's signature semitone trills. These trills are a fantastic way to turn a plain descending arpeggio into something much more exciting, and they'll also give your fingers a solid workout.

Example 2b:

In the next lick, we're diving into a mix of fast trilling legato and slow, expressive bends.

The triplet trills in bars one and two will demand some serious strength from your fretting hand. Don't expect much help from the picking hand here! Focus on keeping your volume, timing, and articulation consistent as you shift positions.

Bars three and four add bends that bleed into double-stops. Played around the first shape F# Minor Pentatonic box. This is a quintessential "rock lead guitar" lick that you'll recognise from countless solos by the greats.

Example 2c:

Moving on to Example 2d, we've got a lick built mostly around two-string arpeggios played with a pull-off technique. Nothing revolutionary, but it's a great way to get comfortable with four- and five-fret stretches while working on your legato clarity.

The real magic here lies in the phrasing and timing. Check out the slide entry at the start of bar one. It's followed by a dotted 1/8th note into a 1/16th note, creating a quirky little "hop step" feel. If this sounds strange on paper, give the audio example a listen and it'll click into place.

Example 2d:

In Example 2e, we're embracing pure chaos with descending triplets. This is all about speed and intensity, so forget melody for a moment and focus on creating a wall of sound.

The lick starts with a repeating whole-step–whole-step shape that adds some position shifts for flavour. In bars three and four, you'll drop into the first shape F# Minor Pentatonic box, sprinkling in Randy's signature "filler" notes (the 2nd, b6, and b5) to keep things interesting.

Example 2e:

The next lick is a tapping extravaganza built entirely around triplet 1/16th notes with a quick double tap thrown in for good measure.

Double taps are one of those flashy tricks that instantly make a lick sound faster and more rhythmically varied. They're also a lot of fun. Once you've got the hang of them, you'll find yourself sneaking them into everything.

Example 2f:

Now let's try Example 2g, where you'll combine trills and an unusual technique that involves yanking a note sharp from behind your fretting hand.

This "no-whammy" whammy trick isn't exclusive to Randy – there's footage of Rory Gallagher doing it years earlier – but Randy definitely brought it into the metal spotlight. Start by pulling a note from a fret behind your fretting hand and watch as chaos ensues.

Example 2g:

(bend with crossover picking hand)

```
full full full full full full full full ½ ½ ½ ½ ½
16-14-16-14-16-14-16-14-16-14-16-14-16-14-16-14   16-14-16-14-16-14-16-14-16-14-16-14-16-14-16-14
```

(bend with crossover picking hand)

```
full full full full full full full full ½ ½ ½ ½ ½
17-14-17-14-17-14-17-14-17-14-17-14-17-14-17-14   17-14-17-14-17-14-17-14-17-14-17-14-17-14-17-14
```

In Example 2h, you'll tackle a fast, two-string triplet arpeggio lick that moves with the chord changes.

This one's all about keeping your picking hand tidy. Start with an up-pick to employ "outside picking" – a technique that'll save you from getting tangled between strings. It's a simple adjustment that makes a huge difference at high speeds.

Example 2h:

Next, we'll combine ascending arpeggios with descending diatonic runs in Example 2i.

The first two bars feature an ascending three-string F# minor arpeggio that leads into a descending diatonic run using the C# Phrygian CAGED shape. Resist the urge to sweep the arpeggio – this lick works best with alternate picking at a steady, mid-tempo pace.

The third and fourth bars follow a similar structure, but with an A major arpeggio ascending into a descending G# Locrian run.

Example 2i:

Finally, let's close things out with a four-note chromatic descending lick. It's played with a mix of legato and palm-muted picking, creating a nice dynamic contrast.

The lick resolves on an ascending A major pentatonic line, punctuated by slides and position shifts. Watch out for the grace note in bar three – it's subtle but adds a lot of character.

Example 2j:

Chapter Three – Edward Van Halen

Edward Lodewijk Van Halen, more commonly known as Eddie Van Halen, was born on January 26, 1955, in Amsterdam, The Netherlands.

Edward's father was a Dutch jazz multi-instrumentalist who encouraged him and his brother Alex (future co-founder and drummer of Van Halen) to study classical piano from a very young age.

At around age 11, Edward picked up the guitar for the first time. He cited Eric Clapton as his earliest source of inspiration and influence, though he was also deeply influenced by the playing of Jimmy Page, Ritchie Blackmore, and Allan Holdsworth. The Holdsworth influence is particularly evident in Eddie's alien-like hand stretches and phrasing.

In his formative years, Edward founded his first band, Mammoth, in 1972 with his brother Alex. By 1974, David Lee Roth had joined the lineup, and the band changed its name to Van Halen.

Van Halen released their self-titled debut album in 1978, often referred to as *Van Halen I*. It remains widely regarded as one of the best hard rock debut albums of all time, cementing the band as one of the greatest rock acts on the planet. The album included the iconic track *Eruption*, which is still often hailed as one of the greatest recorded guitar solos of all time.

The band achieved phenomenal success with their sixth studio album, *1984*. This record showcased their polished songwriting, infectious melodies, and Edward's unparalleled guitar work. It featured timeless hits like *Hot for Teacher*, *Jump*, and *Panama*, which remain classics beloved by fans more than four decades later.

Edward's tone was instantly recognisable and became legendary in the world of rock lore as "the Brown Sound." This harsh yet warm, heavily overdriven tone, often paired with a phaser, had a unique liquidity and depth that guitarists have been chasing ever since.

Eddie was known for using Marshall or Peavey 5150 amplifiers (the latter being his own signature model) and his iconic modded Kramer, the Frankenstrat. By removing the single-coil pickups and replacing them with humbuckers, he created a guitar that redefined the possibilities of electric tone and playability.

Eddie Van Halen forever changed the landscape of electric guitar, much like visionaries Django Reinhardt and Jimi Hendrix before him. He paved the way for countless guitarists, including Nuno Bettencourt, Joe Satriani, John Mayer, Zakk Wylde, Mike McCready (Pearl Jam), and Slash, among many others.

John Mayer, reflecting on Eddie's impact in an interview, once said: "Eddie Van Halen was a guitar superhero. A true virtuoso. A stunningly good musician and composer." It's hard to argue with that sentiment.

Edward's greatest qualities, however, went beyond his playing. His humility and tireless work ethic were as integral to his legacy as his music. He cared more about creating and playing than chasing fame for its own sake. One of his most iconic quotes perfectly sums up his ethos:

"If you want to be a rock star or just be famous, run down the street naked – you'll make the news or something. But if you want music to be your livelihood, then play, play, play, and play! … and eventually you'll get where you want to be."

Recommended Listening

Van Halen – *Van Halen/Van Halen I (1978)*

Van Halen – *Fair Warning (1981)*

Van Halen – *1984 (1984)*

Van Halen – *5150 (1986)*

Van Halen – *For Unlawful Carnal Knowledge (1991)*

All the licks in this chapter will be played over a classic rock-style backing track based around B Dorian/B Mixolydian.

To kick things off, we'll dive into a lick that combines slow triplet bends with a fast legato B Minor Pentatonic run, all played in the first shape. The speed can feel a little daunting at first, but with the right emphasis on legato and economy picking, it becomes much easier to handle. Think of the fast picking sections as mini-sweeps – a sneaky way to glide through the strings without breaking a sweat.

One thing to watch out for is the picking directions. There are two up-strokes in a row, so pay close attention to the notation to avoid any hiccups.

Example 3a:

Next, you'll work on a lick based on percussive, galloping double-stop ideas combined with Eddie's signature ascending tremolo.

The trick here is nailing the shift between muted gallops and the more open double-stops. The muted notes should be tight and controlled, while the double-stops need to pop dynamically to really drive the lick home. In bars one and two, focus on keeping the muted notes quiet while letting the chords ring out with some attitude.

For the tremolo picking in bars three and four, you don't need to aim for perfect 1/32nd notes. Let's be real, counting that fast in real-time is just masochistic. Start with a simple rhythm, like two dotted 1/8th notes into a regular 1/8th, and let the tremolo fill in the blanks naturally.

Example 3b:

```
P.M.------|   P.M.-------------|   P.M.------------------|   P.M.---|
-------------7----------------9--------------------------7--------10--9---7--9-
-------------7----------------9--------------------------7--------10--9---7--9-
---9---9---9-----9---9---9---9---9---------9---9-----9------9---9----------------
```

```
Bar 3: 7-7-7-7-7-7-9-9-9-9-9-9-10-10-10-10-12-12-12-12-12-12-10-10-10-10-10-10-12-12-12-12
Bar 4: 14-14-14-14-14-14-12-12-12-12-12-12-14-14-14-14-17 (full bend)
```

Now let's get into some bent taps and wide-stretch arpeggios.

The bent taps in bars one and two require a ton of control because, let's face it, out-of-tune taps sound awful. Use your first three fingers for strength and stability on the bend, adding a wrist twist for fluidity. The tap itself is more of a flashy afterthought, so don't stress it too much.

In bars three and four, you'll tackle some outrageously wide-stretch arpeggios, inspired by Van Halen's solos in *Ice Cream Man* and *Beat It*. These stretches are brutal, so make sure your thumb placement is on point, or your hand will hate you.

Example 3c:

Example 3d is all about funky dead notes, double-stops, and Eddie's trademark symmetrical scale runs.

The dead notes in bars one and two are essential for that choppy, percussive vibe. Really dig into the strumming and focus on keeping the rhythm tight.

The lick resolves with a legato run, starting on the sixth string and ascending all the way to the first. The 1/16th note triplet rhythm here adds a burst of speed, so keep your legato aggressive and articulate.

Example 3d:

Now let's explore Eddie's take on Chuck Berry-style licks in Example 3e. This starts with a few bent notes that flow into flat-fingered double stops, giving it that classic rock 'n' roll vibe.

The real magic happens in bars three and four, where you'll use tap harmonics, one of Eddie's favourite tricks. The key is to lightly pull your tap back and aim for the centre of the fret, creating a perfect mirrored octave of the fretting-hand melody.

Example 3e:

In the next example, you'll channel Eddie's iconic tapping style heard on *Panama*, *Eruption* and, of course, *Beat It*.

The first two bars focus on triplet taps, which should be as consistent as possible. Be bold with the bent taps too – they're supposed to sound gnarly and full of attitude. If you're struggling to nail the phrasing, listening to the audio example will help a ton.

Example 3f:

This lick is based around a rolling legato pattern on the fretting hand, followed by double and sliding taps on the picking hand.

It starts on an offbeat 1/8th note, so the phrasing might feel a little tricky at first. Listening to the audio will help lock it in. After the chaos of the first two bars, the lick resolves with a slower pentatonic run, featuring 1/8th and 1/4 note triplets for a "calm after the storm" vibe.

Example 3g:

In Example 3h, you'll play a funky, bluesy bending lick based on the fourth shape of B Minor Pentatonic.

The real highlight here is the resolution in bars three and four, which features a diatonic descending pattern with some position shifts thrown in for good measure. Pay close attention to the muted emphasis during the transition. It's a small detail, but it makes a big difference.

Example 3h:

Now let's tap into a B Minor Pentatonic tapping lick in Example 3i.

The fretting hand sticks to the classic first shape box, while the tapping hand adds a fifth interval on each string. The real challenge lies in the third bar, where you'll sweep through a fast three-string Bm7 arpeggio. Eddie used this trick to create surprising and exciting note entries, so take your time to get it right. Don't rush the sweeping motion.

Example 3i:

Finally, we've got a monster lick that crams as many EVH tricks as possible into four action-packed bars.

The first bar features a pentatonic run with legato, pulling off to an open string before jumping to the next string for a jarring b5 interval. The timing shifts between triplet and straight 1/16ths, adding a layer of unpredictability.

In bar two, the tapping lick is nothing new, but the open-note whammy dive deserves special attention. Pluck the open string with your fretting hand, so your picking hand can focus entirely on controlling the whammy.

Bars three and four combine natural harmonics with legato shred. The harmonics follow a simple 1/4 note triplet rhythm, while the legato run uses a wild "sonic shape" with root, semitone, and a 1.5 tone stretch – super fun to play!

Example 3j:

Chapter Four – Kirk Hammett

Kirk Lee Hammett was born in 1962 in San Francisco, California, USA. He got his first guitar at age 15, a Montgomery Ward catalogue special. While functional, its appearance was less than inspiring, resembling something you'd expect to see wielded by heavy metal-themed Lego figures. Kirk eventually upgraded to a 1978 Fender Stratocaster (his personal holy grail), on which he began obsessively honing his craft and developing his signature sound.

In his formative years, Kirk had the privilege of studying under guitar legend Joe Satriani. Reflecting on his time with Satch, Kirk described him as a strict and disciplined teacher, recalling that during his very first lesson, Joe told him,

"Learn your lesson, don't waste your time. Don't waste MY time! I expect you to know everything that I gave you in a week's time."

It's clear that Satriani instilled in Kirk a tireless work ethic and a deep passion for the guitar.

Kirk's early love of music came from his brother, Rick, whose massive record collection featured guitar heroes like Jimi Hendrix, UFO, Stevie Ray Vaughan, and the great Gary Moore. Hammett's love of blues is evident throughout his 40+ year career and continues to influence his playing.

At 16, Kirk formed Exodus in 1979. While the band didn't achieve significant success until after he left, his time in Exodus brought him to the attention of James Hetfield and Lars Ulrich of Metallica. By 1983, Metallica was searching for a lead guitarist to help them complete their debut album, *Kill 'Em All*.

Most bands take time to hone their sound and build a fanbase, often finding success with their second or third albums, but not Metallica. *Kill 'Em All* was met with critical acclaim upon release, with the band's aggressive songwriting, raw energy, and Kirk's electrifying lead guitar work taking the thrash world by storm.

Throughout his career, Kirk has predominantly played ESP guitars, known for their distinctive horror-themed decals. He has occasionally incorporated Fender and Gibson guitars into his arsenal as well.

On the amplifier front, Kirk has favoured Mesa Boogie amps, often paired with an Ibanez Tube Screamer TS-9 pedal and his beloved Dunlop Wah pedals. His KH-95 Kirk Hammett Signature Wah remains a staple of his tone.

It's remarkable that after decades as a member of one of the biggest metal bands in the world, Kirk Hammett has maintained a humble and grounded outlook.

"I didn't want to fall into the trap of competing with all these other great guitar players. I just want to sidestep the whole thing and get out of the race."

This quote perfectly captures Kirk's mindset: focused on playing and creating music rather than competing for recognition. From his teenage years into his 60s, his ethos has remained the same. It's undeniably cool and genuinely admirable.

Recommended Listening

Metallica – *Kill 'Em All (1983)*

Metallica – *Master of Puppets (1986)*

Metallica – *And... Justice For All (1988)*

Metallica – *Self Titled/The Black Album (1991)*

Metallica – *Death Magnetic (2008)*

All the licks in this chapter will be played over a thrashing Metallica style backing track in E Minor/E Phrygian.

To kick things off, let's try a repeating bend lick that combines 1/8th notes with four 1/16th note picks. This carries on for nearly two bars, giving you plenty of time to soak in the thrashy vibe.

The lick resolves with what I like to call a "Kirk descending special," showcasing his love for one-string diatonic runs. You'll pick four notes per beat, but here's the catch: the shapes use three notes per string, meaning you'll need to throw in some smooth position shifts to keep things rolling. This example keeps it concise at one bar, but Kirk has been known to stretch this idea over entire phrases in his solos.

Example 4a:

In Example 4b, you'll play a bending lick in the open position of the E Minor Pentatonic scale. Be warned: these bends near the nut can feel tight, especially if you're aiming for a full step. Don't be shy about recruiting extra fingers for support to stay in control.

The lick finishes with Kirk's signature gallop ascend, played entirely on the third string. The rhythm alternates an 1/8th note with two 1/16th notes, giving you that galloping Iron Maiden feel. Need help locking it in? Try counting "STRAW-BER-RY" with each beat. It works, I promise.

Example 4b:

Now we're diving into a two-string arpeggio sequence, outlining Em, F, G, Em/G, and D/A chords.

The key here is understanding the note groupings, which add a rhythmic twist to an otherwise linear lick. You'll see a mix of 6+6+4 in the first bar and 4+4+4+4 in the second. It might look funky on paper, but listen to the audio and take it slow. Once it clicks, it's incredibly satisfying to play.

Example 4c:

Example 4d starts with an immediate harmonic dive bomb (because why not?) followed by a double-stop pentatonic lick in E Minor.

To pull off the double-stops, use a flat finger to hit the 12th and 14th frets while letting your wrist do the bending and vibrato work. The lick resolves with a Kirk-style triplet pentatonic run, which works best if you think in groups of six. Let the legato carry you through the notes, and don't forget to lean into the swung triplet feel for maximum attitude.

Example 4d:

Next, you'll tackle an ascending pentatonic lick built around the first shape of E Minor. You might recognise this type of run from Randy Rhoads' playbook. It's simple, but packs a punch.

The lick concludes with a 1/16th note legato run grouped as 4+6+6, immediately followed by rolling triplets. The challenge here is handling the subdivision shifts, so study the TAB carefully and listen to the audio to get a feel for the phrasing.

Example 4e:

This idea brings multiple three-string arpeggio sweeps into play, outlining a progression of Em, Em/B, F/C, Em/B, and D/A.

The sweeping motion demands a relaxed picking hand and impeccable coordination with your fretting hand. Don't rush – focus on keeping the triplet swing steady and precise. The TAB includes detailed picking directions to help guide you through the sequence.

Example 4f:

Example 4g explores a few variations of the E Phrygian Dominant scale. You'll start with bursts of legato, 1/16th note triplets to inject some speed into the lick, while the shredded 1/16th notes form the bulk of the melody.

The legato sections prevent the line from sounding too mechanical or "scaley," so let your fretting hand do the heavy lifting to keep things fluid.

Example 4g:

Here's a bluesy double-stop lick that leans heavily on pentatonics. We saw a similar approach in Example 4d, so use flat or barred fingers to nail the double-stops.

The resolution in bars three and four features symmetrical three-note-per-string shapes. They might not stick to strict diatonic rules, but Kirk's "go with the flow" approach makes these shreds sound exciting and dynamic.

Example 4h:

```
Bar 1-2
T---12--------12----------12-----|---12---------12----12---12---
A---12--------12----------12-----|---12---------12----14---12---
B-------14----------14-----------|-------14----------14--------
        (repeated 12/12 and 14 patterns)

Bar 3-4
T--15-14-12--------17-15-14------19-17-15----|--------------22-22-22
  ---15-14-12--------17-15-14-------19------|-17-15---------
  -                                 -        20-19-17-------20-19-17-
                                             full full full
```

This next idea combines legato and open notes to create a playful, offbeat sound. For bars one through three, stick to using just your index finger. It might feel weird at first, but it sets up a smoother transition to traditional pentatonic fingering in the fourth bar.

Example 4i:

```
T--4-0-4-0-4-0-4-0-4-0-4-0-4-0-4-0--|--5-0-5-0-5-0-5-0-7-0-7-0-7-0-7-0--
A
B
```

Lastly, Example 4j features a one-string lick built around Kirk's signature pull-off-to-open-note technique.

The lick is almost entirely made up of 1/16th notes, alternating two legato notes with two picked notes per beat. Pay close attention to the picking directions in the first bar to keep things articulate and clean.

Example 4j:

Chapter Five – Slash

Saul Hudson, better known as "Slash," was born on July 23, 1965, in London, England. He's renowned for his guitar work in Guns N' Roses, Velvet Revolver, and as a solo artist.

At age 15, Slash was gifted a Gibson Explorer copy by his grandmother. Although he had no interest in formal lessons, he dedicated himself to the guitar, often practicing 12 hours a day and skipping school to perfect his craft.

Slash's playing style has always been distinct: loose, rocky, and blues-infused. He credits bands like Aerosmith, Black Sabbath, AC/DC, Led Zeppelin, and The Rolling Stones for sparking his passion for rock music. Among his guitar heroes, Slash frequently praises Keith Richards, Eric Clapton and Jimmy Page, the latter of whom deeply influenced his love for the Gibson Les Paul.

After several high school bands and fizzled projects, Slash met Axl Rose in 1985. Together, they formed Guns N' Roses and, in 1987, released their debut album, *Appetite for Destruction*. Not only was this Slash's first full-length album, but it went on to sell a staggering 18 million copies, solidifying the band's place in rock history.

Throughout his career, Slash has been a loyal Gibson Les Paul player, although he occasionally used the B.C. Rich Mockingbird for solos requiring a whammy bar or a shreddier approach. His amplifier of choice has consistently been Marshall, with his most iconic tone coming from a Gibson Les Paul run through a Marshall 1959T Super Lead or a JCM 800.

Slash's persona has always been as much about humility as it has about talent. Despite his legendary status, he's never claimed to be a technical virtuoso, preferring to focus on songwriting and the collective achievements of his bands. He's known for his cool demeanour and profound, understated observations about music and life.

One of his most famous quotes is,

"Guitars are like women; you'll never get them totally right."

This statement encapsulates his openness to imperfection and his acceptance of the mysteries of both music and life.

Recommended Listening

Guns N' Roses – *Appetite For Destruction (1987)*

Guns N' Roses – *Use Your Illusion II (1991)*

Velvet Revolver – *Contraband (2004)*

Slash – *Slash (2010)*

Slash (featuring Myles Kennedy & The Conspirators) – *Apocalyptic Love (2012)*

All the licks in this chapter will be played over a sleazy rock Slash-style backing track in C Minor/C Dorian.

Let's kick things off with a lick that combines the C Minor Pentatonic scale with diatonic notes and double stops.

One of the trickiest "Slashisms" (yes, that's a word now) to get right is his loose, often delayed rolling legato. In the first bar, you'll notice a staccato 1/16th note that transitions into rolling 1/32nd notes. If the timing feels like a puzzle, listen to the audio provided to unlock the groove.

Example 5a:

Now for an ascending lick showcasing Slash's love of funky double-stops. The initial tritone slide in the first bar implies a C7 chord before easing into more minor leaning double-stops.

This transitions into a classic C Minor Pentatonic lick, solidifying the move from major to minor vibes. Bar three is where the fun (and challenge) begins. Essentially, you're shredding through C Minor Pentatonic in groups of four 1/16th notes. Every note is written as picked, but feel free to sprinkle in some legato if it feels more natural.

Example 5b:

On to Example 5c, where you'll play a slow, bluesy C Minor lick over the first two bars. This part is straightforward, but keeping your bends controlled will require multiple fingers for support.

The magic happens in bars three and four, with a two-string, position-shifting pentatonic lick. Slides and legato are your best friends here. Lean on them heavily to keep things smooth. Pay close attention to the grace notes, as they're more functional for shifting positions than adding melody.

Example 5c:

In this example, you'll descend through a melodic, diatonic passage using a mix of shredding and legato. The shifting between techniques creates some rhythmic intrigue, with the legato sections pushing the note values from 1/16ths to 1/32nds.

This kind of phrasing is quintessential Slash and can be heard on tracks like *Nightrain* and *November Rain*. To fully grasp the vibe, listen to the audio provided and try writing similar licks that explore diatonic scales and subdivision shifts.

Example 5d:

Next up is a position-shifting diatonic run blending shredding and legato.

Slides are essential for transitioning between positions in bars two and three. Skip them at your peril! And those 1/16th note triplets in the second bar? They're fast, furious, and pure Slash. Let the legato do the heavy lifting here. Shredding every note isn't necessary (or sane).

Example 5e:

Here's a mini-etude inspired by Slash's use of motif repetition. Notice how the notation and timing are nearly identical in bars one and two, with the six-note pentatonic legato tail remaining consistent.

The real test comes in bar three, where you'll tackle a single-string, position-shifting legato shred. Slash's unique timing comes into play here, with a staccato triplet 1/8th note leading into flowing legato 1/16th note triplets. The key is nailing the contrast between sharp pauses and smooth runs.

Example 5f:

Now for Example 5g, a bending C Minor Pentatonic lick based around the fourth shape.

For the whole-step bends on the 6th fret of the B string, I recommend using at least two fingers for extra strength and control. This also allows you to add vibrato without it sounding thin or weak.

The lick resolves with a slow, three-string Cm6 and Cm arpeggio – a relatively easy Slashism to emulate. Pay special attention to the shredding, legato, and slides in the fourth bar. Check the audio for guidance.

Example 5g:

This next lick is built around string-skipping inverted 3rds (or major and minor 6th intervals) – a melodic way to tell a story without diving into hyper-speed shredding.

Bars one and two focus on these intervals and will test your string-skipping or hybrid picking accuracy.

Example 5h:

Next, you'll work through a descending 1/16th note pentatonic lick with repeating notes and legato.

Slash uses this trick to create intriguing rhythms and emphasis, both ascending and descending. Watch out for the flat finger double-stops in bar two (a technique we saw in Kirk Hammett's chapter) and the string-skipping inverted 3rds in bar three, as seen in Example 5h. If sight-reading the phrasing feels daunting, hit up the audio.

Example 5i:

Finally, let's dive into Slash's country and southern rock roots with a lick that starts with a three-note unison bent chord in the most common C Minor Pentatonic box. The bend is controlled up and down, setting up one of Slash's signature chromatic licks.

Keep the bends emotional and juicy – don't rush them! If you want to repurpose the chromatic licks, the intervals relative to the root are the 5th, b6, major 6th and b7.

Example 5j:

Chapter Six – Zakk Wylde

Zachary Phillip Wylde, better known as Zakk Wylde, was born on January 14, 1967, in Bayonne, New Jersey, USA. His birth name was Jeffery Phillip Wiedlandt, but he adopted the cooler, rock-ready moniker Zakk Wylde early in his career. On a serious note, can you imagine Ozzy Osbourne introducing a guitarist named Jeffery?

Zakk began playing guitar at the age of 8, but didn't start taking it seriously until he was 15. At that point, he dedicated himself to the instrument, taking formal lessons and practicing relentlessly. His teenage influences included southern rock legends like Lynyrd Skynyrd and the Allman Brothers, as well as the British heavy metal of the 1970s, including Led Zeppelin and Black Sabbath. Zakk has often spoken about his admiration for Ozzy Osbourne's solo career and his reverence for "Saint Randy Rhoads".

By 1988, Ozzy Osbourne was on the hunt for a new guitarist after parting ways with Jake E. Lee. Zakk submitted a demo tape and impressed Ozzy during his first audition. He was invited to join as Ozzy's new recording and touring guitarist. Their first collaboration, the album *No Rest for the Wicked*, showcased Zakk's songwriting and blistering guitar work, going on to sell over 2 million copies.

Zakk and Ozzy achieved even greater success with the release of the 1990 album *No More Tears*, which sold 4 million copies worldwide. The album featured some of Zakk's most iconic solos, including the epic, multifaceted solo in the title track, which perfectly balanced raw emotion with technical precision and speed.

In his early years, Zakk was best known for playing a Gibson Les Paul, famously adorned with a bullseye decal. Later, he partnered with Schecter to produce his own line of flamboyantly designed instruments under the Wylde Audio banner. These guitars were unapologetically bold, with standout designs like the Flying V with SG-style horns.

Like many old-school guitarists, Zakk predominantly uses Marshall amps, particularly the JCM800, paired with a BOSS SD-1 Super OverDrive pedal for added boost during solos.

Zakk has always been known as a genuine musician who loves music and his instrument, without pretence or ego. He once said,

"You've got certain guys that just want to be famous, and then you've got the real musicians that just love playing music."

We can all agree it's best to stick with the latter group!

Recommended Listening

Ozzy Osbourne – *No Rest For The Wicked (1988)*

Ozzy Osbourne – *No More Tears (1991)*

Pride & Glory – *Pride & Glory (1994)*

Zakk Wylde – *Book of Shadows (1996)*

Black Label Society – *This Blessed Hellride (2003)*

The following licks and mini-etudes in this chapter will be played over a black label "Testoster-Rock" backing track in G# Minor.

We'll start with a lick based around the first shape of G# Minor Pentatonic. It combines pull-offs, bends, and shredding, with a touch of shifting subdivisions for good measure.

The real challenge here is the shift from triplet 1/8th notes in the third bar to straight 1/16th notes in the fourth. If this gives you rhythmic whiplash, try practicing with a metronome set at 100, 110, or 120bpm. Alternate between a bar of strict triplet 1/8ths and a bar of strict 1/16ths to lock in the timing before adding melody.

Example 6a:

In Example 6b, you'll ascend through a G# Minor Pentatonic lick using triplet 1/8th notes grouped in six-note patterns over the first and second bars. Pay attention to where the strings are muted for control, versus where they're allowed to ring out.

The lick resolves with a legato-heavy bluesy flourish that leans on double-stops. As we saw in the Kirk Hammett chapter, use flat fingers on the double-stops and add a wrist twist for those juicy bends.

Example 6b:

Next, you'll explore the first shape of G# Minor Pentatonic with bends and legato in the first two bars. The fun begins in bars three and four where chromatics come into play.

For efficiency, stick to three fingers for the chromatic passages and keep your picking hand firmly muting to control any unwanted string noise.

Example 6c:

Here's a lick that fuses pentatonic and diatonic scales. In the first and second bars, you'll keep a bouncy triplet 1/8th note feel – nothing too wild, but rhythmically satisfying. Pro tip: count "pine-ap-ple" for each triplet to stay in the groove.

The third and fourth bars switch gears with a two-string diatonic shred featuring legato. Each six-note grouping begins with a rolling hammer-on, followed by three picked notes. Check the TAB for consistent picking patterns and don't stray!

Example 6d:

Now let's move to Example 6e, where you'll descend through a high-octave G# Minor Pentatonic sequence. This lick features a mix of shredding, legato, and subdivision changes.

The first two bars stick to 1/16th notes, but things heat up in bars three and four with triplet 1/16th notes. While it may seem straightforward, the two-note-per-string pentatonic shapes demand precision and incremental speed-building, especially when shifting subdivisions.

Example 6e:

The next lick is a position-shifting concept moving from the fifth to the first shape of the G# Minor Pentatonic scale. You can tackle most of this lick with just two fingers, but keep a couple of extra digits handy for bends requiring more support. Make it sound bold and confident – there's no room for timid playing here.

Example 6f:

In Example 6g, you'll focus on multiple double-stops within G# Minor Pentatonic. The first two bars start with a flat-fingered roll emphasising 1/16th note triplets.

If, like me, your pinkie is about as reliable as a soggy noodle, switch to your ring, middle, and index fingers for those rolls. The lick resolves with a descending run from the fifth to the first shape, broken into groups of four 1/16th notes. Stick with just two fingers to keep it clean.

Example 6g:

This next idea introduces three-note arpeggios played across two strings, creating a fast looping pattern.

The tricky part? Every repetition flips the picking pattern. Pay close attention to the picking directions in the first bar to avoid tangling your fingers into oblivion.

Example 6h:

Here, you'll play the G# Minor Pentatonic scale with a splash of southern rock major 3rd, and some tasty tapping.

As always, let your fretting hand handle all the bending and vibrato. The second bar's bend is entirely fretting-hand-driven with the tap added gently from above.

The third bar's trills echo those from Example 2c in the Randy Rhoads chapter. Keep your volume and articulation consistent. In the fourth bar, a symmetrical pattern across the first and third strings ends with taps. The audio example is your friend when it comes to nailing the phrasing.

Example 6i:

To close out this chapter, you'll play through G# Minor Pentatonic in a high octave using an ascending three-note motif with a 1/16th note pulse. The lick intensifies with triplet 1/16th notes in the second bar.

Switching between subdivisions adds unpredictability, transforming a straightforward line into something more engaging. To master the jump, set your metronome to 100bpm and alternate between two bars of dead 1/16ths and two bars of triplet 1/16ths.

Example 6j:

Chapter Seven – Marty Friedman

Martin Adam Friedman, better known to fans as Marty Friedman, was born in 1962 in Washington, D.C., USA. After attending a KISS concert at the age of 14, Marty became determined to play guitar, write songs, and start a band immediately. His unconventional mindset and drive led him to bypass formal training altogether – a decision that shaped his unique note choices and idiosyncratic picking technique, likely a result of being entirely self-taught.

Marty's musical influences were wildly eclectic, ranging from the Beach Boys to Black Sabbath. He also credited The Ramones, KISS, and Mahogany Rush as pivotal inspirations in his early years.

At 15, just one year after picking up the guitar, Marty joined a band called Deuce. Although his time with the band was short-lived, he went on to form Hawaii in 1981. During their four years together, Hawaii released two EPs and two full-length albums.

By 1986, after Hawaii disbanded, Marty teamed up with a young shred prodigy, Jason Becker. Together, they formed Cacophony, a band that masterfully blended complex heavy metal shredding with classical composition. The two albums they released during their time together continue to influence the shred guitar world to this day.

Cacophony disbanded in 1989, leaving Marty a free agent. In 1990, after a successful audition, Marty joined Megadeth as their lead guitarist. Becoming part of one of the world's most successful thrash bands propelled him to fame. His virtuosic guitar work on Megadeth's 1990 album, *Rust in Peace*, cemented his status as a household name among metal and shred enthusiasts.

Marty's tenure with Megadeth was incredibly fruitful, particularly with the 1992 album *Countdown to Extinction*, which sold over 2 million copies.

In his early Megadeth years, Marty was often seen playing a Jackson Kelly guitar, which became closely associated with his image. These days, he's more likely to be seen wielding his signature PRS or Jackson models, both of which resemble the classic Les Paul shape.

Since his departure from Megadeth in 2000, Marty's sound and tone have evolved significantly. ENGL amps and BOSS multi-effects units play a central role in his setup. His focus has shifted toward creating intricate and heartfelt guitar melodies that replace the traditional role of vocals and lyrics, allowing his playing to tell a story.

Marty's approach to guitar and songwriting has always been quirky and unconventional. He claimed to have rushed through the basics and avoided learning others' music as much as possible, preferring instead to write songs from the outset.

His humorous and unapologetic ethos is perfectly encapsulated in this quote:

"Even if you screw up, you just claim that the song is written like that and no one can challenge you."

Recommended Listening

Cacophony – *Speed Metal Symphony (1987)*

Marty Friedman – *Dragon Mistress (1988)*

Megadeth – *Rust In Peace (1990)*

Megadeth – *Countdown to Extinction (1992)*

Marty Friedman – *Inferno (2014)*

Due to Marty's diverse style (and him being my favourite guitarist) he gets special treatment. I've composed two backing tracks with different feels, each with five licks.

The first five example licks will be played over a happy Japanese ballad backing track in the key of E Major.

Let's kick things off with a lick based on an E major arpeggio spanning two octaves. On paper, this is a straightforward triad over two-and-a-bit octaves, but what makes it Marty-esque are the slid grace notes, position shifts, and moments of legato. Make sure you pay close attention to the fingering I've suggested in the first bar.

The lick resolves with a C# minor arpeggio, played with an 1/8th note triplet feel and some of Marty's signature position shifts. Be mindful of those slides, they're your secret weapon for making position changes seamless and smooth.

Example 7a:

Next up, we have a lick that mixes a descending horizontal diatonic idea with a happy-sounding pentatonic scale (yes, happy pentatonics are a thing).

The first two bars feature 1/16th note triplets and 1/32nd notes for a rhythmically interesting line you can play entirely on a single string. If the phrasing or timing trips you up, listen to the audio provided.

The lick resolves on a C# Minor Pentatonic line. What gives it Marty's signature sound is the descending run, which starts with a wider interval and stretch, throws in a b5 for tension, and finishes with an outside-to-inside bend. Take your time on the slow bend at the 10th fret – it creates a lovely bit of tension before you hit your target note.

Example 7b:

Now let's move on to Example 7c. This lick is a simple melodic line that works horizontally across two strings. The "special sauce" lies in the backslide entry in the first and third bars, as well as the slower, more emotive bends that create tension and release.

If you're struggling to lock in the phrasing, listen to the audio for those sweet Marty-esque nuances.

Example 7c:

This next idea is built around a two-string pentatonic lick that emphasises string changes, economy picking, and perfect 4th intervals.

The focus here is the flat-finger roll played with economy picking in the first two bars. Keep an eye on the notation to see where those swept up-picks happen, and don't skimp on the detail – it's what gives this lick its unique feel.

Example 7d:

Now for a lick that combines an interval-skipping E major arpeggio with a C# Minor Pentatonic line.

The arpeggio's notes can bleed together if you're not careful, so controlling your muting and flat-finger rolling are essential.

The highlight comes in the second bar with a stretch from the 9th to the 14th fret. This isn't crazy hard, but it does demand good thumb placement. Try positioning your thumb at the 12th fret on the back of the neck to make the stretch manageable.

Example 7e:

Now we shift gears with five licks played over a "Rust in Shred" thrash metal backing track in E Minor/E Phrygian.

Here's a lick that revisits the flat-finger rolling economy picking technique from Example 7d, but this time in a vertical E Minor Pentatonic box.

Make sure you follow the notated picking directions. Those rolls need to be smooth and precise to nail the feel.

Example 7f:

In Example 7g, we dive into two classic Marty tropes: the Hirajoshi scale and position-shifting arpeggios.

The first two bars are mostly 1/8th notes with a few bursts of legato triplet 1/16th notes. It's straightforward, but sounds more complex thanks to the legato (trickery like this is peak Marty).

The last two bars introduce shifting arpeggios. Once you've got the sequence under your fingers, focus on staying one step ahead – you'll need to anticipate those position shifts to keep things clean.

Example 7g:

This next lick is an octave melody played on the first and third strings. It builds tension without relying on overly complicated passages or flashy technique.

Bar three includes some string skips, so hybrid picking might be worth trying if you find traditional string skipping awkward. As always, choose what works best for you!

Example 7h:

In Example 7i, you'll work through a repeating sequence that alternates between an ascending E major arpeggio and a descending E Phrygian Dominant scale run.

The arpeggio isn't fast enough to warrant sweeping, so use alternate picking. For the scale run, lean on the legato sections – they'll give your picking hand a break and add some dynamic variance to the descending phrase.

Example 7i:

We'll finish with a lick that uses the E Hirajoshi scale, legato, and an outside-to-inside bend.

Take your time on the bend in the second bar – it's Marty to the core when you milk that outside note before resolving to the inside target note. The lick resolves with a position-shifting F major arpeggio, leading into a chromatic run. Use the grace note slide to nail the position shift and set you up for the chromatic shred. For maximum efficiency, use all four fingers of your fretting hand.

Example 7j:

Chapter Eight – Nuno Bettencort

Nuno Duarte Gil Mendes Bettencourt, born in 1966 in the Azores, Portugal, is best known for his jaw-dropping guitar playing and songwriting in the rock band Extreme.

As the youngest of ten children (yes, ten!), Nuno grew up surrounded by music, often looking up to his older siblings. His brother Luís, a highly skilled guitarist, became a significant influence, lighting the spark for Nuno to begin his guitar journey at the age of 12.

An unashamedly self-taught guitarist, Nuno honed his skills by relying on his ears, natural rhythm, and musical instincts. He drew inspiration from guitar greats like Edward Van Halen for his buttery-smooth legato technique, and Al Di Meola for his Latin-infused, percussive approach to staccato shredding.

Nuno had a brief stint in a band called Sinful before joining and forming Extreme in 1985. By 1989, the band released their self-titled debut album *Extreme*, packed with catchy choruses, killer solos, and just enough glam to make them a standout in the metal scene.

Nuno's career spans collaborations with an impressive array of artists, including Janet Jackson, Rihanna, and stadium-rock behemoths Nickelback. However, Extreme saw their greatest success with the 1990 release of their sophomore album *Pornograffiti*, which sold nearly 3 million copies and solidified their place in rock history.

In 1990, Washburn teamed up with Nuno to design the now-iconic N4 Signature model guitar – a weathered, relic-like super-strat that oozes personality. Nuno still plays updated versions of this guitar today, proving that if it ain't broke, you just tweak it slightly and keep rocking.

Over the years, Nuno's amps have ranged from Randall to Fender, Marshall to Hughes & Kettner, and even Soldano. But the not-so-secret weapon in his rig is his Ratt pedal. This beast punches up his tone, giving his rhythm playing a percussive, kick-drum-like quality that shines in heavily muted riffs. Just listen to *He-Man Woman Hater* for a masterclass in Nuno tone.

Nuno's playing has earned high praise from some of the most accomplished guitarists in the world. Steve Vai, Tom Morello, Mateus Asato, Zakk Wylde, and Steve Lukather (of Toto fame) have all sung his praises. But perhaps the most noteworthy compliment came from one of Nuno's childhood heroes, Brian May, who perfectly summed him up:

"There's plenty of fast, accurate guitarists, but what he brings to it is this amazing spirit. It's energetic and lyrical."

From his larger-than-life, rock star stage persona to his laid back, brutally honest demeanour in interviews, it's clear that Nuno loves what he does, and he does it with passion, vulnerability, and a relentless work ethic.

If there's one piece of advice Nuno lives by, which all musicians should take to heart, it's this:

"As much as you put in is as much as you get out!"

Amen!

Recommended Listening

Extreme – *Extreme (1989)*

Extreme – *Extreme II: Pornograffiti (1990)*

Extreme – *Waiting for the Punch Line (1995)*

Nuno – *Schitzophonic (1997)*

In order to create context, I've composed a backing track for all the licks in this chapter based on an Extreme-style funky glam metal groove in G Minor/G Dorian.

In the first lick, you'll play some funky double-stop bends in the first shape of G Minor Pentatonic. I'd recommend holding the 6th fret on the second string with your pinkie while using the rest of your fingers to focus on controlling the pitch and ensuring those whole step bends sound tight.

The third bar is where things get spicy. Pay extra attention to the placement of the 1/8th note triplets mixed in with 1/16th note triplets. This funky little hop-step rhythm is classic Nuno and crucial for nailing his vibe. If the groove feels elusive, have a listen to the audio provided to hear the lick in context with the backing track.

Example 8a:

Next, you'll tackle a lick built around Bbadd9 and Cadd9 arpeggios, using a mix of legato, string skips, and taps. This requires two notes per string on your fretting hand, with a tapped note added by your picking hand.

Keep an eye on the tapping sequences on the high E string for both arpeggios and aim for sniper-level accuracy on the string skips. The lick resolves with a G Minor Pentatonic idea that leans on the Dorian major 6th sound. Watch out for those bends and grace note slides – they drastically affect the delivery. If the phrasing proves challenging, I'd suggest wearing out the replay button on the audio example.

Example 8b:

Here's a muted diatonic lick combining shredding, legato, and a heavy palm mute. The first three bars stick to similar timing and motifs, pulling fragments from the G Dorian (or F Major) scale.

In the final bar, we shift gears and shred through an ascending, three-octave A Phrygian run. Ditch the palm mute here to let the notes breathe and build toward a big, climactic bend.

Example 8c:

Now for a signature Bettencourt stretch: a three-note diminished arpeggio on each string. These stretches are no joke, so keep your fretting hand thumb aligned with your middle finger. If you line it up with your index finger, you're in for a world of pain!

The lick resolves with tremolo picking blended with legato – a great way to create tension and build up speed before wrapping up a solo.

Example 8d:

```
T|--15-18-15-12-15-18-15-12-----15-12--------12---|--15--18--15--12--15--14--13------------13--------|
A|-------------------------18---------18-15-----18-15-12-|------------------------------15--12------15----(15)--|
B|                                                      |                                                   |
       3                       3                            3


T|--6--6--6--6--6--6--6--6--6--6--6--6--5--6--5--3--------3--6--5--6--5--3--------3--6--|
A|------------------------------------------------------6------------------------6-----|
B|                                                                                    |
   3      3      3      3              3                 3
```

```
T|--10--10--10--10--10--10--10--10--10--10--10--10--9--10--9--6--------6--10--9--10--9--6--------6--|
A|------------------------------------------------------------------8--------------------8-----|
B|                                                                                            |
     3      3      3      3              3                      3
```

In Example 8e, you'll loop a fast-paced G Minor Pentatonic lick that leans on symmetrical shapes, the b5 interval, and legato technique.

The first two bars are identical, so focus on maintaining consistent legato speed. You may also find it easier to stick to just your index and ring finger for these bars.

Example 8e:

This lick builds around triplets using the G Minor Pentatonic scale, borrowing a stylistic motif from Extreme's *Play With Me*. The first two bars are blazing fast, so let the legato technique do most of the heavy lifting.

The lick resolves with a simple one-string tapping idea, finishing on a bent tap.

DISCLAIMER: Do not bend or add vibrato with your tapping hand. The bend comes entirely from your fretting hand, and your tapping finger should politely join the party afterwards.

Example 8f:

The next example begins with a diatonic, string-skipped run. The first bar uses legato to help you gain speed, while the second bar opts for strict alternate picking. Although the note intervals remain consistent, the switch-up in techniques makes this scalar run sound more dynamic and engaging.

The lick wraps up with a chaotic tremolo section outlining a G minor arpeggio. Precision isn't the priority here; a slightly messy, rock-style tremolo can sound raw and exciting. Eddie Van Halen has proven this time and again in solos like *Eruption, Somebody Get Me a Doctor* and *Beat It.*

Example 8g:

This lick features a repeating motif with subtle variations in the second bar. The first pentatonic phrase resolves to the tonic, while the second shifts to a major 7th, adding a harmonic minor flavour (sometimes called the Pentalodic scale!)

This approach can work over complex chord changes or evoke a nostalgic Brian May vibe.

SIDENOTE: For a deeper dive into the Pentalodic scale, check out my book *Exotic Scales for Rock Guitar Soloing*.

Example 8h:

This next lick emphasises the funky, Dorian elements of the backing track by incorporating Gm7 chords with frequent appearances of the major 6th (E).

It's all about nailing the 1/16th note rests and dead notes. Listening to the audio example will help you lock in these details.

Example 8i:

The final lick combines legato, alternate picking, and open strings. The first two bars feature classic pentatonic tropes like double-stop bends, outside major 3rds, and b5 intervals.

Things heat up in the third bar with 1/16th note triplets played entirely on the third string. This section mixes fretted notes, open strings, and position shifts – a melodic trick you'll recognise from solos like Extreme's *Play With Me* or riffs like AC/DC's *Thunderstruck*.

The lick concludes with a tapping idea that rolls forward and backward with the fretting hand. Pay close attention to the TAB and the audio example to master this flashy ending.

Example 8j:

Chapter Nine – Dimebag Darrell

Darrell Lance Abbott, better known as "Dimebag Darrell" was born in 1966 in Ellis County, Texas, USA. Early in his career, during Pantera's lesser-known glam metal phase, he went by the nickname "Diamond Darrell", but by the early 1990s, as the band shifted to a heavier, groove-orientated sound, he adopted the moniker "Dimebag Darrell", which he used for the rest of his career.

Dime took up guitar at the age of 12, inspired by bands like KISS, Black Sabbath, Judas Priest, and the legendary Eddie Van Halen. According to lore, the first song he learned was Deep Purple's *Smoke on the Water* and he and his brother Vinnie jammed it for six hours straight. This was the spark that ignited Dimebag's passion for music, guitar, and eventually forming the early iterations of Pantera with his brother.

Thanks to their father, Jerry Abbott, a producer with a home studio, the Abbott brothers recorded Pantera's debut album *Metal Magic* in 1983, when Dime was just 16 and Vinnie was 19.

Throughout the 1980s, Dimebag gained a reputation as a musical prodigy and local celebrity. He dominated guitar competitions so thoroughly that organisers eventually banned him from entering to give others a chance. As a consolation, Dime was invited to judge future contests, keeping him involved while sparing other contestants the humiliation of competing against him.

Despite Dimebag's jaw-dropping skills and accolades, Pantera remained relatively obscure throughout the '80s. Everything changed in 1990 when the band overhauled their sound and recruited Phil Anselmo's aggressive vocal style. The result was *Cowboys From Hell*, an album brimming with iconic riffs, killer solos, and undeniable energy. It sold over 2 million copies, catapulting Pantera into global metal stardom.

Dimebag was known for his devotion to Dean ML and Washburn Stealth guitars – both similarly shaped instruments that became synonymous with his image. He helped popularise both brands within the metal scene and even sported a signature Washburn design with a confederate flag paint job.

His gear played a pivotal role in crafting his signature sound. Dime used Randall amps, a signature Crybaby Wah, and a DigiTech Whammy pedal, paired with his mastery of divebombs and double-tracked rhythms and solos. These elements defined the tone that countless metalheads fell in love with during their teenage years.

Although Pantera began in the '80s, Dimebag's legacy and influence truly spanned just over a decade, starting with the release of *Cowboys From Hell*. Many musicians regard Dimebag's impact on metal as comparable to the revolutionary waves Eddie Van Halen made in rock music.

Dimebag's accolades are a testament to his influence. *Rolling Stone* ranked him No. 92 on their "100 Greatest Guitarists of All Time" list, while *Guitar World* placed him at No. 9 in a similar ranking in 2012.

He was also honoured with an induction into Hollywood's RockWalk by one of his heroes, Ace Frehley. These recognitions gave peers and fans alike a chance to celebrate Dimebag's contributions to heavy metal.

Jonathan Davis, the vocalist of Korn, once said, "He was one of the greatest guitar players ever. I mean, if there was no Dimebag Darrell, there would be no Korn."

Dimebag's career and personality were shaped by his unconventional approach to music and life. He was a rule breaker from the start, as perfectly summed up by one of his quotes:

"The worst advice I ever received was from my dad, which was to play by the book."

Recommended Listening

Pantera – *Power Metal (1988)*

Pantera – *Cowboys From Hell (1990)*

Pantera – *Vulgar Display of Power (1992)*

Pantera – *Far Beyond Driven (1994)*

Damage Plan – *New Found Power (2004)*

For this chapter, I composed a backing track to create context and capture the Dimebag essence. All ten examples in this chapter are played over a Pantera-style groove metal backing track in the key of D Minor.

First up, we have a lick that combines attitude-soaked bends and pentatonics with a splash of chromaticism. The coolest part happens in the third and fourth bars, where the usual pentatonic formula of 1, b3, 4, 5, b7 gets spiced up with chromatic interplay between the b7, major 6th, and b6 intervals.

Check out where they occur in the notation and pay close attention to the legato emphasis and picking directions in the TAB.

The lick resolves with a legato roll that briefly dips into that southern rock major 3rd sound Dimebag loved.

Example 9a:

Next, we have a symmetrical shape Dimebag adored, made up of a root, semitone, and a stretch of 1.5 tones. To survive this shape, keep your fretting hand thumb lined up with your ring finger to make the stretch bearable.

The lick wraps up with some whammy tricks featuring dive bombs and harmonics. As with Eddie Van Halen's approach, pick the note with your fretting hand and let your picking hand focus entirely on controlling the whammy bar's expression.

Example 9b:

Let's dive into a blues-rock flavoured lick that starts with a familiar entrance, seen in previous chapters (Slash, Kirk, and Zakk would approve). What makes this uniquely Dimebag is the sliding major and minor 3rd intervals in the third and fourth bars.

There's plenty of position shifting here, so take it slow and always stay one step ahead of yourself visually on the neck.

Example 9c:

In Example 9d, we get a repetitive rolling D Minor pentatonic lick that leans heavily on the b5 and uses plenty of legato. Don't get carried away with the speed! Stay locked into the 1/16th-note pulse and keep your timing consistent across the first two bars.

Example 9d:

This lick is a masterclass in Dimebag's love of chromaticism. Stick to a strict four finger, four fret approach to keep your fretting hand efficient and evenly balanced.

While the fourth bar isn't purely chromatic, maintain the four finger setup for consistency. I've included suggested fingering in the notation to help you out.

Example 9e:

The next line spans multiple positions of the F Major or D Minor scale, taking inspiration from the closing run in Pantera's *Domination* solo.

The notes themselves are fairly straightforward, but the lick is played as 1/16th note triplets at blistering speed. Keep the pulse consistent and consider using just the first two bars as a warmup before tackling the whole phrase.

Example 9f:

In Example 9g, we kick off with tremolo picking and some wide hand stretches on the first and second strings. Keep your picking hand wrist loose and fluid while aiming for accurate timing and clean notes.

The third and fourth bars move into a traditional vertical D Minor Pentatonic box with a few extra notes from a neighbouring position grabbed by a stretched pinkie. Watch out for tricky picking patterns and legato emphasis. Pay close attention to the TAB for guidance.

Example 9g:

Next up is an ascending symmetrical shred pattern that transitions into a descending symmetrical legato pattern.

The shred in the first two bars takes inspiration from Dimebag's love of Ace Frehley. While it has a pentatonic flavour, the inclusion of the b5, major 6th, and 2nd creates a three-note-per-string shape that's perfect for shredding. You might be tempted to use your pinkie, but I stick to my index, middle, and ring fingers for this one.

The legato section in the third and fourth bars requires a significant stretch. Keep your thumb aligned with your middle finger and position your fretting hand on the back of the neck to handle the reach.

Example 9h:

In Example 9i, you'll play a mix of chromatics and slides across a diagonally ascending pentatonic shape. Pay special attention to muted notes and position shifts to keep everything clean and articulate.

Example 9i:

Finally, we have a lick that combines bent taps, pentatonic tricks, and ascending spooky tritone intervals.

As always with bent taps, the fretting hand handles all the bend and vibrato work – don't try to bend with your tapping finger!

The third bar features a two-string pentatonic lick with bends and legato. Use economy picking where possible to keep the string changes smooth and seamless.

The ascending tritone phrase in the fourth bar works best if you stick to just your index and middle fingers, up until the 20th fret bend. This lick constantly changes phrasing, so I recommend listening to the audio example for guidance.

Example 9j:

Chapter Ten – Synyster Gates

Brian Elwin Haner Jr., better known to Avenged Sevenfold fans as "Synyster Gates" was born on July 7th, 1981, in Long Beach, California. As the son of Brian Haner Sr., a musician, comedian, and author, Synyster clearly inherited his father's creative genes.

At the age of 10, Syn's father began teaching him guitar. But Syn quickly tossed the rulebook out the window, insisting they skip scales and theory entirely in favour of learning Led Zeppelin classics like *Black Dog* and *Stairway to Heaven*. This may not have been the traditional approach to learning guitar, but it was certainly effective, igniting Syn's passion for the instrument. And let's be honest, aren't we all glad his dad gave in?

Synyster's influences are as eclectic as they come. He cites gypsy jazz legend Django Reinhardt and fusion maestro Allan Holdsworth as major inspirations, but he also grew up worshipping heavy metal icons like Eddie Van Halen, Slash, Dimebag Darrell, and John Petrucci. These diverse influences helped shape the signature fusion of technical prowess and melodic sensibility Syn is known for today.

Syn took his playing to the next level by studying under two fusion greats: T. J. Helmerich, famous for his eight-finger tapping technique, and Australian virtuoso Brett Garsed.

Before fully committing to Avenged Sevenfold, Syn experimented with a side project, Pinkly Smooth, alongside drummer Jimmy "The Rev" Sullivan. Although short-lived, the band allowed Syn and The Rev to hone their skills before they both joined Avenged Sevenfold in 2001. That same year, the band released their debut album, *Sounding the Seventh Trumpet*.

After grinding it out for a few years, Avenged Sevenfold shot to stardom with their 2005 release, *City of Evil*. The album showcased the band's songwriting chops and Syn's jaw-dropping guitar solos, helping to cement their place in the metal world. The album was a commercial success, selling over 2.5 million copies worldwide and earning the band a loyal following.

For nearly his entire career, Syn has been a die-hard Schecter player. His go-to guitars include the *Synyster Gates Custom-S* and the *Schecter Golden Goddess*. With fast necks, ergonomic cutaways, and Sustainiac pickups, these guitars are perfectly tailored for shredding, dive bombs, and endless sustain.

On the amp front, Synyster's sound evolved from the Mesa Boogie Dual Rectifier to his signature Schecter Hellwin Stage 100. Both amps deliver the punchy, rock-infused rhythm tone and silky smooth leads that define his playing.

Syn is revered for his ability to blend elements of country, blues, gypsy jazz, and metal into his solos. Avenged Sevenfold stood out as a band unafraid to embrace technical guitar work during the early 2000s, a time when many metal bands were ditching solos entirely in favour of nu-metal's stripped-back style.

Despite his undeniable talent, Syn has always maintained a down-to-earth attitude and a deep respect for music. One of his most poignant quotes sums it up perfectly:

"Music is a beautiful thing to listen to. It is not a thing to preach to others about, it's not a cause. It is what it is, and that's a beautiful art form."

Recommended Listening

Avenged Sevenfold – *Waking the Fallen (2003)*

Avenged Sevenfold – *City of Evil (2005)*

Avenged Sevenfold – *Nightmare (2010)*

Avenged Sevenfold – *Hail to the King (2013)*

To give all the examples in this chapter some melodic context, I've composed a backing track with a theme of Avenged Syn-rock-metal in the key of D Minor.

Let's kick off with a simple arpeggio line, played at a slow, deliberate pace using 1/4 note triplets and a cheeky chromatic enclosure with a gypsy flair.

If you're struggling with the rhythm, grab a metronome and practice playing 1/4 note triplets with a simple scale or exercise. Once you've nailed the timing, listen to the audio provided to hear how it locks in with the backing track.

Example 10a:

The next mini-etude gradually ascends through D minor and G minor arpeggios, both written as 1/8th note triplets. While the arpeggio shapes themselves aren't particularly difficult, the pattern involves plenty of string hopping, so watch out for notes bleeding into one another, especially in the first and third bars. Keeping it clean is key!

Example 10b:

Now let's move on to Example 10c, where you'll combine arpeggios and diatonic runs played entirely on the first and second strings.

This one is pretty straightforward, but you'll want to focus on the placement of the legato passages in the third and fourth bars. They add flow and melodic interest, so don't gloss over them!

Example 10c:

The next idea is built around a repeating motif in the first and second bars. Each bar includes two bends followed by three 1/16th note triplets.

The trickiest part is transitioning between legato and shredding. The middle triplet in each bar features a legato roll, while the surrounding notes are played with staccato precision. If this gives you trouble, practice just the transitions in isolation before working them back into the full lick. Listen to the audio for extra clarity.

Example 10d:

Example 10e mixes sweeping and tremolo-style picking.

In the first and second bars, you'll play an arpeggio crossing three strings that outlines a D minor triad with the addition of the 2nd (1, 2, b3, and 5). While this section is written as 1/32nd notes, don't worry too much about perfection. Think of it as two dotted 1/8th notes followed by a regular 1/8th note, then shred it like there's no tomorrow.

The sweeping arpeggios in the third and fourth bars should feel familiar. Practice these sections separately to ensure your hand synchronisation and note clarity are spot on.

Example 10e:

The next lick uses symmetrical shred patterns across the first and second bars. This approach lets you create a fast, impressive line without worrying about sticking to diatonic notes or staying in key (rules are for squares, right?)

This is a rapid-fire lick, so you'll probably need some intense metronome drilling. Try practicing in groups of six (two 1/16th note triplets per click) to build up speed and control.

Example 10f:

Now we'll explore a simple four-note arpeggio that is essentially a minor triad with the addition of a 2nd (1, 2, b3, and 5).

The lick itself isn't too difficult if you're familiar with the required fingerings and position shifts. Pay extra attention to the suggested fretting-hand fingering in the first and third bars for smoother transitions.

Example 10g:

The next lick begins with a slow melody that transitions into a G minor arpeggio played with a skipping interval sequence. This might feel a bit awkward, so take note of the recommended fretting-hand fingering in the notation.

If hybrid picking makes the arpeggio or subsequent string-skipped legato phrase easier, feel free to give it a shot!

Example 10h:

Here you'll combine trills, arpeggios, and four-note-per-string chromatics.

In the first bar, the trills outline a D minor arpeggio. While these are notated as 1/16th note triplets, the goal is to play them as fast and cleanly as possible.

The second bar features a four-string F major sweep that transitions into an alternate inversion on three strings. The subdivisions shift from 1/16th notes to triplet 1/16ths, so be prepared for a sudden burst of speed.

The chromatics in the final bars may remind you of classic finger warm-ups. This section isn't about melody, it's about chaos! Play it robotically and as accurately as possible to amplify the madness of the lick.

Example 10i:

We'll finish with a lick that combines pentatonics, chromatics, and arpeggios for maximum speed and chaos.

Keep your fretting-hand fingers close to the fretboard to make the back and forth rolling motions during the shred sections more fluid.

The arpeggios themselves (D minor and Bb) are just basic five-string triads, so you've got this!

Example 10j:

Conclusion

Well, here we are at the end of the book! If you've made it this far, congratulations, you've survived a whirlwind tour of legendary guitarists, their quirks, and their sometimes painfully difficult licks. Whether you're shredding pentatonics like Zakk, blending classical flourishes *à la* Randy, or trying not to sprain your fretting hand on one of Marty's stretches, I hope you've found inspiration (and maybe a few calluses) along the way.

What have we learned? Well, aside from the fact that most of these guys couldn't resist a Marshall and signature guitar combo, we've seen that every player brings their own unique flair to the instrument. Kirk has his gallops and dramatic bends, Eddie brought tapping and tremolo to the masses, and Slash… well, Slash proved that sunglasses are essential PPE to wear while melting faces.

This book wasn't about trying to turn you into a carbon copy of your heroes, it's been about learning from them, stealing their tricks (legally, of course), and finding ways to make them your own. Whether it's throwing in a southern rock major 3rd for some Dimebag spice or hitting a Slash-inspired double-stop with your wrist doing all the work, you now have a buffet of licks to feast on. Just don't mix them all into one solo unless you really want to confuse your audience.

Most importantly, I hope this book has reminded you why you picked up the guitar in the first place. Maybe it was to write the next great riff. Maybe it was to impress someone who couldn't care less about modes. Or maybe you just saw someone on stage and thought, "I want to do that!" Whatever your reason, never lose sight of the fun.

Now go forth, crank your amp to an antisocial volume, and write some music that would make these legends proud. And if you can't nail that Marty Friedman legato run on the first try, don't worry, he probably didn't either!